BECOME A PART-TIME PROFESSOR

Live and teach anywhere you like

Published in the United States
By New Way Press
www.newwaypress.com

ISBN-13: 978-1502818058
ISBN-10: 1502818051

Why this book?

Being a part-time professor can bring you prestige and enhance your resume for career growth. It is a way for you to give back and teach the next generation what you have learned through hard work and dedication. Many people say that when they started teaching at a university, they found their passion.

If you picked up this book, you are probably considering becoming a part-time professor. My name is Lesa Hammond and I have over 15 years in higher education. I have been a staff member, an administrator, a guest lecturer, and an adjunct faculty member. I have worked in five different colleges and universities, from one of the largest public universities, to a community college, to small or medium size private universities. And one thing that I found all of them have in common... *finding qualified part-time faculty is a challenge*.

Connecting colleges and universities with qualified adjunct faculty has been an ongoing challenge. The company ProfHire will provide a full range of services for both the higher education institutions and adjunct faculty.

If you are interested in teaching part-time at a university, this book will give you an insider's understanding of the job and what it takes to get it.

Table of Contents

Introduction

Have you ever considered teaching college courses or wondered if you have what it takes to be a professor in your field of expertise? In this little book, you will not only learn if you have what it takes, you will learn what you can do to get what it takes and you will learn the secrets of getting one of those coveted titles people call "professor."

We live in a time where you can live anywhere in the world that you can imagine. For some people the only thing holding them back is thinking about bringing in enough money to sustain their current lifestyle.

Baby boomers are increasingly considering living abroad in order to maintain their lifestyle, reduce expenses and finally live the luxurious life they have only glimpsed during a one and two week vacation.

Unfortunately, many baby boomers are continuing to work into their 70s because they don't have enough money to retire. For many, an extra $1000 or $2000 a month would allow them freedom from that nine-to–five (or nine-to-nine) job. By teaching part-time, they could leave that full-time job.

There are artists, writers, researchers, and entrepreneurs who love the flexibility of living wherever they want. Some choose to live in the United States on a mountain, while others live in remote parts of the world. Still others spend their time on cruise ships or exploring the globe. Many of these people have one thing in common—one source of their income is teaching college courses at American universities. If this lifestyle interests you, this book will show you how you can live it.

This book is written to be a reference for you as you think about and begin the process of looking for your part-time university teaching position. This book contains a lot of references and website links. If you purchased a physical copy of the book you will have an opportunity to receive a free copy of the ebook.

The part-time professor

When you hear the term professor does it conjure up images of the "Nutty Professor" or of an absent-minded professor?

Or maybe the image of a brilliant intellectual comes to mind.

Either way, today, the college professor could be the woman or man next door. College professors have full lives and a lot of expertise in a specific field. Are you an expert in a certain career field or is a niche in your business where you have more knowledge than most other people in your field?

Let's see if you have what it takes. A "yes" answer to any of the following could qualify you for a job teaching college level classes.

Yes	No	
		Do you have expertise in a specific field?
		Do you have advanced training?
		Do you have a graduate degree?
		Have you written a book?
		Do you have a popular blog or write magazine articles?
		Have you reached noteworthy success in your profession?

Answering "yes" to even one of these questions may qualify you to teach a college course or two.

Most colleges and universities only hire people who have advanced degrees unless they have very significant or unusual knowledge in a specific career field.

A professor without a PhD

Most colleges and universities require a masters or doctoral degree to teach college courses; however, that's not always the case. Looking at the various types of higher education available, the degree requirements can be quite different based on the type of school, level of education attained at the school, and the reputation of the school itself.

No Degree or Associates Degree

If you do not have a degree, your chances of teaching at a college are remote, but you might still be able to teach in a **trade or vocational school**.

George is an example of someone who doesn't have a college degree, yet teaches at the local media arts school. George attended two years of college, but dropped out to move to California and follow this dream to work in Hollywood. When he arrived in LA he met a man who offered to teach him a trade. George has now been working as a sound technician for ten years. He has met the A-List of the rich and famous. Because of George's industry knowledge, he is able to teach part-time in a college for media arts. Trade schools will often hire individuals who have an associate degree or bachelor degree and significant experience in the trade. With some trade schools, it is more about what you know than the degree you hold.

Trade or vocational colleges include schools that exclusively focus on art and design; culinary arts; allied health professions (dental assistant, laboratory technician, x-ray technician, etc.); business (bookkeeping, administrative assistant, legal assistant, etc.); skilled trades (HVAC, plumbing, electrician, aviation, automotive); and beauty and cosmetology.

If you think you might want to teach in a trade school, CLICK HERE to get a list.

Bachelors

Community colleges or junior colleges generally require a masters degree. However a bachelors degree can be acceptable if the candidate for the position has significant experience or expertise, or is in a field where few people get a degree beyond the bachelors.

Christina didn't speak a word of Spanish until she went to a Spanish immersion high school. She then majored in Spanish in college. As an undergraduate, she studied abroad for one semester in Mexico and another semester in Argentina. Christina did not continue to get a masters degree but her experience, fluency in Spanish, and bachelors degree landed a part-time faculty position teaching Spanish at the local community college.

Community colleges also have some of the trade school programs. In those cases, the same criteria that applies to trade schools applies to the community college and a person without a bachelors degree can teach in these programs.

Masters

Undergraduate degree programs almost always require their faculty to have a minimum of a masters degree. Individuals with specialized skills or expertise may on a rare occasion be hired as part-time faculty. It is more common for these programs to bring people with specialized skills into a classroom to provide a lecture than it is for them to be hired to teach the full course. However, individuals with masters degrees are frequently hired to teach at the undergraduate level.

Terminal and Doctoral Degrees

A terminal degree is the highest degree generally awarded in a field. The MFA (Master of Fine Arts) and MBA (Master of Business Administration) both have doctoral options, however these are not offered at many schools and the MFA and MBA are considered terminal degrees.

Unless you are working at a school that offers the DBA or DFA, you can teach any level course in that field including graduate level courses. Schools that offer DBAs and DFAs often have difficulty finding faculty with the appropriate credentials to teach their classes.

A doctoral degree is considered the highest attainable degree. Yes, there are people who have post-doctoral degrees, and most of them are already faculty or headed directly to a tenure-track position.

Part-time professor by any other name

The term part-time professor is "popular language" so to speak. In the "Academy[1]" part-time professors are called a number of things, and "part-time professor" is generally not one of them. The rank of *professor* is actually the highest rank a faculty member can achieve without special commendation. The most common title for a person who is hired to teach one course at a time is **adjunct faculty**. The United States Department of Education uses the title part-time faculty.

A part-time professor or part-time faculty usually refers to someone who teaches on a per course basis. That means when a course in your field of expertise is needed you are asked to teach that course. There is no guarantee of teaching, nor is there a guarantee of a salary. Adjuncts are hired on a per course contract basis.

Depending on the college or university where you are working, you might hear the following terms: adjunct, adjunct faculty, part-time faculty, lecturer, and guest lecturer. Schools

---

[1] Although the term <u>Academy</u> can be used to refer to any collective of colleges and universities, it generally refers to four year institutions that offer under-graduate and graduate level degrees.

create their own titles for the people who teach part-time. Some call them visiting professors, but then again, visiting professors are often tenured[2] or core faculty who come from other universities. There is also the term contingent faculty, which depending on the university, may teach full-time but not be tenured or core faculty.

In 2002, Michael Shamous, of Carnegie Mellon University looked at the overwhelming array of titles given to university faculty. His list appears in the HANDBOOK ON ACADEMIC TITLES.

---

[2] Tenure is an arrangement whereby faculty members, after successful completion of a period of probationary service, can be dismissed only for adequate cause or other possible circumstances and only after a hearing before a faculty committee. This is designed to ensure academic freedom.

Keep in mind that this was done in 2002 and the list may have morphed a bit, but not much.

The only reason it is important for you to know the variety of titles that could be given to part-time professors is so that you can recognize an opportunity when it comes your way.

Here is the list of the many titles that might appear when you are looking for a part-time faculty position:

- *Adjunct / Adjunct faculty* (most common)
- *Adjunct professor*
- *Affiliated faculty / Affiliate professor*
- *Annual faculty* (often used for full-time one year appointments)
- *Casual Appointment* (commonly used term in Canada and Australia part-time teaching positions)
- *Contingent faculty* (can be used for part-time positions and other non-tenure track positions)
- *Contract faculty* (generally hired for a term or year, sometimes multiple years, may be part-time or full-time.)
- *Faculty-in-residence* (may be given to certain specialized personnel, e.g. artist, scientist, or scholar, appointed on a part-time or full-time basis for a term or an academic year.)
- *Guest Lecturer* (speaks to a class because of his/her expertise, is paid a flat rate, and is not the instructor of record)

- *Instructor* (may or may not be part-time and usually denotes a person without a terminal degree)
- *Interim Faculty*
- *Lecturer* (sometimes used for part-time and sometimes full-time faculty, but it indicates someone who is not eligible for tenure)
- *Limited-term appointment / Limited-term faculty*
- *Per course faculty*
- *Pro-rata faculty* (generally per course faculty)
- *Professor adjunct* (this is actually an esteemed position because it is a ranked position based on previous teaching or expertise. e.g. Assistant Professor Adjunct)
- *Visiting faculty / Visiting professor* (usually someone who is tenured faculty at another university. A few institutions use this title for part-time per course faculty)

Yes, it is a long list and surely you didn't read through the whole thing; but it's a good reference if you ever see a job and you wonder if the job matches your needs and qualifications.

The phrase "part-time professor" is commonly used by people who don't work in higher education; you will almost never hear anyone referred to as a "part-time professor" at a college or university. For the purposes of this book, I will use

New faculty majority

According to the American Association of University Professors (AAUP) the number of part-time faculty increased from 30.2 percent in 1995 to 48 percent in 2005. An article in The Atlantic magazine stated that adjuncts constitute 76.4 percent of United States faculty[3].

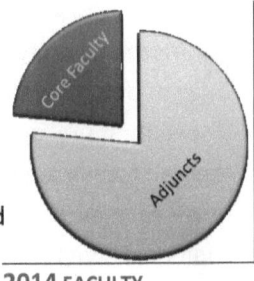

2014 FACULTY

What does this mean?

If you are looking for a part-time job as a college professor, it means that there are more and more opportunities available. It also means that the face of higher education is changing and if you take the part-time job in hopes of it becoming a full-time job, your chances of that happening a slim.

Part-time faculty used to be hired for basically two reasons: first, as a temporary replacement for a faculty member who was on sabbatical or some other form of leave; and second, to bring practitioners in a field into the classroom to provide real-life information and experiences. Today, part-

---

[3] This information is attributed to the AAUP and appeared in an April 28, 2014 article in *The Atlantic*.

Why become an adjunct?

The decision to teach at the college or university level is obviously a personal one. People who are adjuncts often chose to take a part-time teaching position because they love to teach. On a recent Oprah Classic on XM Radio, Oprah made a comment to one of her guests, "Don't you just love teaching?" (Oprah teaches a leadership class at Northwestern University's Kellogg School of Management.)

If you don't enjoy teaching, this is not the profession, even on a part-time basis, for you. Even if you enjoy teaching, your love of molding young (and old) minds may not be your primary reason for taking an adjunct position. There are a variety of equally legitimate responses to the question, "Why become an adjunct?"

Deciding to teach part-time at the university level will have multiple advantages. I have identified the four P's as the primary reasons you would choose to take a part-time faculty position:

Prestige

Being a part-time professor can enhance your reputation and credibility.

Robert has written over a dozen books including one that hit the New York Times Best Seller list years ago. When he retired from his government job, he turned to screenwriting full-time and also began teaching graduate level screen-writing courses. His adjunct faculty positions made him standout when talking with others in the Entertainment Industry.

Purpose

Reina is a stay at home mom. Teaching English classes online keeps her skills up-to-date and gives her some extra spending money.

Passion

Fay was a high school art teacher. When she left her job to pursue her own art full-time, she continued her passion for teaching by being an adjunct professor at an American university while living overseas. Sometimes she teaches online and at other times she teaches face-to-face. This allows her flexibility as she travels the world.

Pay

Adjunct salaries vary depending on a number of factors, including:

- The discipline;
- The university;
- The region of the country where you live and teach;
- The degree level;
- The length of a course (courses range from two weekends to 16-weeks).

The chart below gives a rough idea of what you might expect in 2014:

DISCIPLINE	PAY / COURSE
Trade Schools / Community College	$1200 - $2000 associate degree level
Liberal Arts (English, foreign languages, art, journalism, education, etc.)	$1500 – $2800 undergrad. $2000 - $3500 graduate

DISCIPLINE	PAY / COURSE
Business (Economics, Accounting, Marketing, etc.)	$2000 - $3500 undergrad. $3000 - $6000 graduate
Professional (Law, Medicine, Engineering, etc.)	$3200 - $8000 graduate only

A final factor in the pay rate is whether or not the school provides the full curriculum or if you have to design your own course.

Contingent faculty were never meant to be full-time professors. The expertise of contingent, affiliate or adjunct professors comes from their practical experience.

One of the hot topics in academia today is the pay adjuncts make. Some feel that they are not making the salary they deserve. However, if they recognize the benefits of working as a part-time professor, they will see that the pay is only one benefit.

There are books and programs out there that say a person can make $100,000 as an adjunct professor. While technically this is true, the person who teaches enough to make $100,000 as a part-time faculty member is probably teaching twenty or more classes a year.

Most people who work as part time professors do not think of it as a full-time profession.

If you are looking at a full-time faculty position, the requirements are generally quite different. The ideal part-time faculty member brings practical experience to the classroom.

Understanding adjunct pay

Former CIA Director, General Petraeus makes $200,000 teaching a 3-unit course at CUNY. On the other hand, you may have heard stories of adjuncts on food-stamps, HOMELESS, and DYING IN POVERTY. If you are looking to find out the salary of part-time professors, you can find some pretty extreme examples.

So what's the real story?

The average salary of a part-time professor per course is between $1500 and $5000.

In most universities, a credit-hour or unit roughly equates to the number of hours in class per week. There are of course exceptions with schools that have a different assignment of time/unit, but for our purposes, it won't make a difference.

As a result of the AFFORDABLE CARE ACT, the IRS quantified the time required to teach a course. In February 2014, the approved time multiplier of 2.25 hours for every hour a faculty member is in class was ratified as the official guideline for higher education institutions. Given this formula a part-time faculty member teaching a 3-unit course will be credited with 6.75 hours our service per week; therefore if you are teaching a 15-week semester, that would be 6.75 x 15 or 101.25 hours of work per semester.

The typical part-time faculty position pays between $1500 – $5000/ college course. For the purposes of explanation, let's assume you make $2500 for teaching a 3-unit course for 15 weeks. Based on the 2.25 formula, you would make $24.69/hour. That rate includes your time in class, office hours, preparing, and grading papers. Some weeks you will work more than 1.25 additional hours for each hour in class and other weeks you will work fewer.

According to the AMERICAN ASSOCIATION OF UNIVERSITY PROFESSORS (AAUP) 2013 data, the average salary of a full-time assistant professor nationwide is $58,406. Adjusting for inflation at 1.5% per year, the 2014 median salary would be as high as $59,282. Based on a work week of 40 hours, the assistant professor working full-time would be paid for 12-months at a rate of $28.50/hour. Based on a 9-month contract, the median rate for a full-time Assistant Professor is $37.05/hour.

Who makes a good adjunct?

Adjunct faculty come from all walks of life. They are professionals, entrepreneurs, solo-preneurs, the semi-retired, and retirees.

Margaret and Phil are retired and live a quiet existence. They love teaching their online courses from their easy chairs. "It feels like we are sharing our work," says Margaret. Even though Margaret teaches English and Phil teaches a math class, they enjoy their time together as they teach.

Entrepreneurs and solo-preneurs make excellent affiliate faculty if they know how to teach. They are able to work their schedule around their classes and share extremely up-to-date expertise about their profession with their classes.

Individuals who work in a specific profession or industry can bring real life experience and situations to the classroom that all of the theory in the world will not inform.

A good adjunct is not only about the field or profession from which the person comes, but the personality, the desire to teach, and the willingness to engage with students.

Live anywhere and teach

Do you live in a remote part of the United States where there aren't many, or any, universities in the area? Maybe you live or plan to move abroad? You can teach college courses.

Did you know that more than 6.7 million students—32 percent of total higher education enrollment—took at least one online course through a university during fall 2011; and studies show that that number is steadily rising. To emphasize the expansion of online courses, 62.4 percent of the 2500 colleges surveyed in 2012 offered fully online degree programs. That number is up from 32.5 percent in 2002, according to the report.

It seems obvious that if a course is completely taught online, as long as you have internet access you are available to teach the course. However, online courses are not your only option. If you would rather teach a face-to-face, classroom based course, you'll be happy to know that if you are near a US military base in another country, there will most likely be a university presence and they could very well need faculty. You can also teach abroad at a university owned and operated by a United States university.

According to GLOBAL HIGHER EDUCATION, April 2014 statistics show that there are 50 United States universities and branch campuses[4] in more than 80 countries, and this not a comprehensive list. The UNIVERSITY OF MARYLAND UNIVERSITY COLLEGE runs programs out of many military bases and has a European and an Asian branch, and the COLLEGE OF NEW JERSEY has graduate programs in Spain, Thailand, Portugal, Taiwan, Vietnam, South Africa, and Egypt.

As you can see, if you want to teach, there are plenty of opportunities, but you have to know where to look and how to get your foot in the door. You can go to PARTTIMEPROFESSOR.COM to get advice and search for available adjunct positions.

When looking for a teaching position at a United States university, you may need to maintain your U.S. passport, a U.S.

[4] See Appendix I

postal address, and bank account. Laws pertaining to right to work in the United States have not caught up to the global nature of work in the age of the Internet.

Your curriculum vitae

If you are from any country other than the US, you might call any document that shows your work history a curriculum vitae. In the U.S., a resume and a curriculum vitae or CV are quite different. The current trend is for the resume to be succinct and accomplishment based. The fewer pages the better. However, that trend has not caught on with higher education. When applying for a teaching position in a university, longer is often better. Your curriculum vitae should contain the following[5]:

---

[5] Reproduced with permission of Adjunct HR, LLC.

Education - Your level and field of education are the first two things that will be noticed on your CV. If you do not have the right education for the courses you are applying to teach, your chances of getting the job drastically diminish. So, first look for jobs in your field of study and work. Most colleges and universities requires at least a Masters degree for faculty unless you are renowned in your field.

Teaching Experience - Have you taught classes? Anywhere? Even if you have taught K-12 or run seminars, these experiences count. The more you have been up in front of people and shared your knowledge the better prepared you are to teach at the college level.

Online Teaching Experience - If you are applying to teach online courses, any experience you have had teaching online is fantastic. If you have not had experience teaching online, your experience taking online courses is helpful. If you don't have either, we will be developing an online instructor training program that you can take. In the meantime, you may want to find an online course at a community college just to get the experience of participating in such a course before applying to teach one.

Other Work Experience - One of the greatest assets adjuncts bring to colleges and universities is their practical work experience. The practitioner in a field brings insights that the career professor may not have. Sometimes there is no substitution for being out in the field and doing the job.

Publications - In higher education, peer reviewed articles hold the most weight; however any published articles in any journal, magazine or even an online publication should be listed. If you have written a book, again books by academic publishers receive the most respect, then books published through traditional publishing companies, and finally self-published books are worth listing. If you haven't published anything, don't worry many adjunct faculty have no publications under their belt.

Research - Research is generally only required for core faculty and then it is only required in some fields and some universities. However, if you have conducted research make sure that you list it.

Presentations - If you have delivered speeches or been on panels at conferences or other public events you want to list to name of the presentation, the event, the location (city, state, country) and the month and year.

Committee and Organization Work – List any committees you are on with your current employer. If you were the Chair, Secretary, and Treasurer or held some other position on a committee, list that. List any nonprofit board on which you sit. And list any professional organizations where you are a member.

If this seems a bit overwhelming, there is a worksheet at the back of the book for you to begin putting everything in one place. Once you do that, formatting is all that is left. If you don't know how to format your CV, PARTTIMEPROFESSOR.COM provides resources for you.

You may be used to writing your resume and while your resume is pretty impressive, this CV is a bit intimidating. What can you do if you haven't written any books or taught any classes?

Fortunately, as an adjunct you aren't expected to have the same amount of teaching experience, research, and publications as tenure track or core[6] faculty. You are however expected to have a good grasp of academia and be connected in your professional field.

If you really do not have enough to make a CV look presentable, you have two option:

---

[6] Core Faculty - refers to all faculty both tenured and non-tenure who are generally full-time and at a minimum have multiple year contracts.

1. Create a resume that will provide an excellent overview of your strengths and write a strong cover letter. If you have never taught, never written anything, not done any presentations, nor conducted any research, you might want to get busy doing some things to enhance your CV, but in the meantime you can use your resume. HTTP://BLOCKBUSTERRESUMES.COM is a free ebook on how to create a great resume

2. Use the CV format and emphasize the Work History section, but add to the other sections as much as possible.

One major difference between a resume and a CV is that the CV is not as time-based as the resume. With a resume, you generally will not go further back than 10 years. With a CV your professional and academic accomplishments can span your entire career. However, keep in mind, going too far back in history and noting accomplishments earlier than the late 80s ages you. As an adjunct, that may not be a bad thing. Your wisdom and historical perspective may be considered an asset depending on what courses you aspire to teach.

BABY BOOMERS BEWARE

Although your extensive work history and accomplishments might be impressive, if your CV looks like a throwback from 1980, you will drastically reduce your opportunities. Your wisdom and experience will only be valued if you look like you have stayed current with modern technology. If your CV looks like it was created on a typewriter you will lose the chance to make a good first impression.

Teach online

It used to be that every university wanted to hire people who already knew how to teach online. Today, most universities have online introductory training for new faculty. The truth is that there are many platforms being used and each one is unique. The most common are BLACKBOARD and MOODLE, however many schools have their own platform or have customized the standard platform so much that you cannot go from one school's online platform to another without getting some training.

Generally, when you take an online teaching job, at a minimum you will receive coaching from an individual who will explain how to use all of the features. Some universities will require you to take a course that can last from two to eight weeks depending upon their training process.

However, if you have never taken an online course, you might consider signing up for one so that you can experience the online platform from the perspective of the student. I think you will find it quite beneficial to know what works and what doesn't for you as a student. It will also give you the opportunity to understand how the course feels for the students. I find that this particularly helps instructors understand the need for giving timely feedback, what good feedback looks like, and the importance of pacing the course.

The course you choose to take doesn't really matter, but take one that you will finish. You can take a course at your local community college. You can take a MOOC[7] from one of the many free course websites. You will notice that there is generally a lot of material developed for each course. Don't be intimidated that you will not be able to develop that much material. If selected to teach a class, will likely be guided through developing your material or it is becoming more common for schools to provide the course material for online courses.

---

[7] MOOC stands for Massive Open Online Courses. MOOC are free to take but in order to get credit for the course the student must pay.

Here are some resources for finding free online courses that you can take:

HTTPS://WWW.COURSERA.ORG/COURSES

HTTP://OEDB.ORG/OPEN/

HTTPS://WWW.EDX.ORG/

HTTP://WWW.OPENCULTURE.COM/FREE_CERTIFICATE_COURSES

Online courses are generally identified as asynchronous[8] or synchronous[9]. Most courses are in an asynchronous format, allowing people all over the world to take the course without having to wake up at in the middle of the night or interrupt their work schedule to attend the class.

If you are teaching an online course, you may have people from every corner of the earth taking your class. I recently taught an online course with only 10 students and they were from five states of the United States, Canada, Brussels, Egypt

---

[8] Asynchronous – students can go into the course 24 hours a day to post their assignments. The instructor responds. It's like when you use Facebook and different people respond at different times.

[9] Synchronous – this is less common because it requires everyone to log on at the same time. This is often used with webinars, video conferences and teleconference. It can be used with a chat feature.

and Bahrain. English was not the first language of three of the students. Online courses offer a wonderful opportunity for students and instructors to see just how small this globe has become and how easy it is for all of us to connect.

Teach on the go

Remember universities from the United States are holding classes all over the world. The best thing about online classes, is not only will you teach students from around the world, and you can teach them while traveling the world.

Joanne retired from the military after 20 years. Although she is not near retirement the normal retirement age, she prioritized travel as the most important things in her life. She teaches online classes to fund her excursions and teaches the classes while on them.

Whether your goal is to teach while sailing the world or sitting on a beach, online teaching can provide you the freedom to be where you want to be while teaching your courses.

When traveling or living abroad make sure you have an excellent Internet connection.

Some colleges and universities are hesitant to allow people living or traveling outside of the United States to teach courses, because of the issues with Internet connectivity. If you plan to teach online, while living or traveling overseas, sailing the ocean, or relaxing on a remote island, make sure you have a good Internet provider.

One of the quickest ways to ruin your online teaching career plans, and for you to potentially ruin them for others, is to go MIA on your students because your Internet didn't work. Even though online teaching allows for an immense amount of flexibility and freedom, it is still a job and you are responsible for your students' education.

If you plan to travel while your class is in session, it would be a good idea to have your class set up before you leave, double and triple check Internet access, and have a contingency plan in the event your best laid plans fail.

Your first time teaching online or even teaching a new class, It is recommended that you stay in one place where you are familiar with your Internet access. You also want to have a back-up plan if things aren't working. A local internet café is always a good back-up. Also, if this is your first time teaching online, make sure that you are able to connect with the university during their business hours. Even though the online class is 24-hours a day, that doesn't mean that the university's support staff works those hours.

Semester at Sea

If you love the thought of standing in front of a classroom and getting those visual clues from your students, then you may want to teach classes on-site. Face-to-face classes are referred to as "brick and mortar," "on-ground," or sometimes they are simply referred to as in a "classroom."

Even if your preferred teaching method is face-to-face there are many options, which still allow you to teach throughout the world.

Semester at Sea

Semester at Sea is an amazing program that allows college students to take one semester and travel the world. The students take college classes while on the ship and when they dock at port they experience the various cultures of the world.

Acceptance as a Semester at Sea faculty member is a competitive process and elite position. It is not for the new instructor. If you have international experience, a terminal degree, and have already taught in a university, this is one way to take your experience and see the world.

If you don't fall into the group above, you might qualify for a staff position. Check out the various opening available at:

HTTP://WWW.SEMESTERATSEA.ORG/DISCOVER-SAS/OUR-ORGANIZATION/EMPLOYMENT/

Jim, directed the audiovisual department at a college. He applied to oversee the audiovisual department at Semester at Sea. Jim traveled the world three times on the floating campus.

A full semester on the open seas may sound a bit overwhelming to you. If so, you might be able to participate in one of the excursion trips which lasts about four weeks. The competition to teach on a Semester at Sea voyage is tough, so you will want to plan this very early. For more information on Semester at Sea requirements for teaching go to:

HTTP://WWW.SEMESTERATSEA.ORG/

This is not a Royal Caribbean cruise. It is a college campus on water. You will live with approximately 1000 college students for a full semester. But if you are up for it and you have the credentials, this could be an exciting adventure.

Never taught before

If you have never taught a class before, depending upon your expertise and the school's need, you might land a job without any teaching experience. In general, it would be beneficial for you to get some experience before applying for jobs. Each situation is unique. Significant public speaking experience could take the place of classroom experience.

Recently, many colleges and universities have instituted instructor training and prepared lesson plans and syllabi. Without teaching experience, it will be easier to get your foot in the door at one of these universities. However you probably will not know which schools offer such a program, so cast your net wide. Apply for both online and classroom teaching positions at as many schools as you possibly can.

One way to overcome the lack of teaching experience is to make presentations. Contact your local professional organization and make a presentation at a meeting. Develop a presentation for a professional seminar or conference.

Apply to teach an extended education course. Extended education programs are available at many universities. These are generally non-credit courses that do not lead to a degree, but may lead to a certificate. Some of the courses are academic in nature and other are just for fun. You could also go to your local community college or community center to propose a course to teach through their extended education programs.

Go to PARTTIMEPROFESSOR.COM for additional tips and help writing your CV. If you do not have experience teaching, a very well-crafted CV can demonstrate the skills you possess.

Create an online course

If you have a specialized skill or knowledge, you can create your own online course. There are several programs that provide a platform for you to create your own course.

Creating your own course has multiple advantages. First, you are not waiting for a university to hire you. You can begin to develop an alternate income stream and you can take the course with you wherever you go. Second, when you create an online course that is self-directed, you have a residual income stream and you can make money while you sleep (or travel).

There are so many stories of successful online courses where people have made over six-figures. Though it may sound like a get rich quick scheme, it isn't. The competition for online courses is tough because more and more are available.

However, if you have a unique skill or knowledge, you could be successful. Your ability to market yourself will drastically increase your chances of success. There are a number of platforms where you can create a course for free. They also provide free training on how to create a course. Websites like UDEMY AND SKILLFEED.COM allow you to put your course online for free and they simply receive a portion of your sales.

Creating your own online course also serves as a portfolio of your teaching ability and knowledge.

FAQs

What if I've never taught before?

If you have never taught a class, create a CV and see where the gaps are. If your only gap is teaching, get other experience in front of groups and sharing your knowledge. Workshops, presentations, and the like may be fine substitutes for actually teaching a class.

What is my time commitment?

In most universities, the number of units is determined by the hours per week that you will be in class. For example a 3 unit class would require you to be in the classroom three hours per week. When you first start teaching a course the time commitment outside of class will be significant. If you have to create the course it is even more. Just getting started and getting your bearings takes time. After you have taught the course a few times, you will find that it becomes less time consuming and more enjoyable. Online classes typically take less time than face-to-face classes, if for no other reason than you don't have to drive to the location.

What's the worst part of being a part-time professor?

Most adjuncts complain about having to grade papers and say that is the worst part of the job. It is certainly one of the most time consuming parts of the job.

How do I get started?

Start by creating a CV using the format provided in this book. Then see if there are gaps that need to be addressed. After you have a CV that adequately demonstrates your experience and knowledge look for jobs. You can go to PARTTIMEPROFESSOR.COM and look for jobs and post your resume. HIGHEREDJOBS.COM is also a good site for searching for jobs.

Where can I find more information?

Go to PARTTIMEPROFESSOR.COM for more information and sign-up for the helpful tips.

What if I want to be a fulltime professor?

Adjunct faculty positions seldom lead to fulltime faculty appointments. Becoming a fulltime tenured or core faculty member is highly competitive, and the trend in higher education is moving further and further away from fulltime tenured positions. The average salary for a beginning fulltime tenure-track faculty member is $50,000 - $60,000. The requirements for core faculty members include ongoing scholarship (research and publishing), service (committee work, special projects), attending meetings, events, and more. The most common route to becoming a core faculty member is to begin the process while still attending college. Most start as exceptional students, then become teaching assistants and research assistants, and finally land a core faculty position after graduation.

What if I want to teach at a foreign university?

This book is written for people teaching at U.S. universities. Over time, PARTTIMEPROFESSOR.COM will offer information about teaching in other countries.

Helpful resources

PARTTIMEPROFESSOR.COM Currently you can get help with your CV and will do a CV review. You can also search for adjunct faculty positions. CONTACT US for additional resources.

LERN offers certifications for teaching online and some classroom certifications. You may not need this type of training, but if it makes you more confident, it might be worth it.

NEW WAY PRESS is a collaborative publishing company that specializes in educational, inspirational and transformational books. If you have a book you seek to have published, this is one resource. It is a mix between self-publishing and traditional publishing.

UDEMY allows you to create your own course content.

HIGHER ED JOBS is a job board for all jobs in higher education including administration, and full-time and part-time faculty jobs.

U.S. universities abroad[10]

Institution Name	Host Country
Alliant International University	Mexico
American Intercontinental University	United Kingdom
Arkansas State University	Mexico
Baruch College, City University of New York	France
Baruch College, City University of New York	Singapore
Baruch College, City University of New York	Taiwan
Berklee College of Music	Spain
Boston University Institute for Dental Research and Education	United Arab Emirates, Dubai
Boston University	Belgium
Brookdale College Ecuador	Ecuador
Carnegie Mellon University	Australia
Carnegie Mellon University	Greece

[10] List gathered from *Global Higher Education* April 2014
HTTP://WWW.GLOBALHIGHERED.ORG/BRANCHCAMPUSES.PHP

Carnegie Mellon University	Qatar
Carnegie Mellon University	Rwanda
Carnegie Mellon University, USA	China
Institution Name	**Host Country**
City University of Seattle	Bulgaria
City University of Seattle	Greece
City University of Seattle	Slovakia
City University of Seattle	Switzerland
Clark University	Poland
Cornell University- Weill Medical College	Qatar
Culinary Institute of America	Singapore
DeVry University	Canada
Digipen Institute of Technology	Singapore
Duke University	China
Empire State College	Albania
Empire State College	Czech Republic
Empire State College	Dominican Republic

Institution Name	Host Country
Empire State College	Greece
Empire State College	Greece
Empire State College	Lebanon
Empire State College	Panama
Empire State College	Turkey
Endicott College	Mexico
Fairleigh Dickinson University	Canada
Florida State University	Panama
Fort Hays State University	China
Institution Name	**Host Country**
Fort Hays State University (FHSU)	China
Fort Hays State University, USA	China
George Mason University	South Korea
George Mason University – Campus turned into American University of RAK	United Arab Emirates, Ras Al Khaimah
Georgetown University School of Foreign Service	Qatar
Georgia Institute of Technology	France
Gonzaga University	Italy
Houston Community College	Qatar

Institution Name	Host Country
Hult International Business School	United Arab Emirates, Dubai
Hult International Business School	United Kingdom
Johns Hopkins University	Italy
Johns Hopkins University, US	China
Kean Univeristy, US	China
Keiser University (formerly Ave Maria University)	Nicaragua
Lakeland College	Japan
Lynchburg College	St. Lucia
McDaniel College	Hungary
Michigan State University	United Arab Emirates, Dubai
Missouri State University, USA	China
Monroe College	Saint Lucia
New York Film Academy	United Arab Emirates, Abu Dhabi
Institution Name	**Host Country**
New York Institute of Technology	Bahrain
New York Institute of Technology	Canada
New York Institute of Technology	Jordan

New York Institute of Technology	United Arab Emirates, Abu Dhabi
New York Institutte of Technology	China
New York University	United Arab Emirates, Abu Dhabi
New York University Shanghai	China
New York University Tisch School of Arts	Singapore
Northwestern University	Qatar
Parsons - The New School for Design	France
Potsdam, The State University of New York	Canada
Rochester Institute of Technology	United Arab Emirates, Dubai
Saint Louis University	Spain
Savannah College of Art Design	China (Hong Kong SAR)
Schiller International University	France
Schiller International University	Germany
Schiller International University	Spain
State University of New York - Stony Brook	South Korea
Stevens Institute of Technology	Dominican Republic

Sylvan	India
Temple University	Japan
Institution Name	**Host Country**
Texas A&M University	Israel
Texas A&M University	Qatar
The University of Chicago Booth School of Business	Singapore
The University of Chicago Booth School of Business	United Kingdom
University of Indianapolis	Greece
University of La Verne	Greece
University of Michigan, USA	China
University of Nevada, Las Vegas	Singapore
University of Nevada, Las Vegas	South Korea
University of New Orleans	Jamaica
University of Phoenix	Canada
University of Phoenix	Mexico
University of Pittsburgh	China
University of Pittsburgh, USA	China
University of Utah	South Korea

Virginia Commonwealth University	Qatar
Webster University	Austria
Webster University	Ghana
Webster University	Switzerland
Webster University	Thailand
Webster University	The Netherlands

CVWORKSHEET

Name: _____

Address: _____

Email: _____

Cell phone: _____

Education

List your degree, university, major, and dissertation or thesis topic. You highest attained degree is first.

_____

_____

_____

University Experience

List as you would on a resume, any academic or administrative positions you have held in a university. This is not where you will list the courses you have taught.

_____

_____

_____

_____

_____

Other Work Experience

List your other work experience. One of the greatest assets adjuncts bring to colleges and universities is their practical work experience. Unlike with a resume, you can go back beyond 10 years if the experience is pertinent to the courses you are applying to teach.

_____

_____

_____

_____

_____

Teaching Experience

List any teaching experience you have. This is where you will list the courses you have taught and the years. List every course including course numbers. If you are a high school teacher you can list the subjects.

_____

_____

_____

_____

_____

Online Teaching Experience

Any experience you have had teaching online is fantastic. You can either parenthetically state (online) or list online classes as a separate category.

_____

_____

_____

_____

Publications

In higher education, peer reviewed articles hold the most weight; however any published articles in any journal, magazine or even an online publication should be listed. List publications in MLA or APA format - Here is a good website for correctly formatting your books, magazines, and online articles HTTP://WWW.CITATIONMACHINE.NET/.

_____

_____

_____

_____

Research

If you have conducted research make sure that you list it. Even research you did as a part of your job might count if it included a research methodology or statistical analysis and you have results to show for it.

_____

_____

_____

_____

_____

Presentations

If you are not keeping a list of the various presentations you do, start now. Think back and list every possible presentation you can remember. If you have delivered speeches or been on panels at conferences or other public events you want to list to name of the presentation, the event, the location (city, state, country) and the month and year.

_____

_____

_____

_____

_____

VIEW A FORMATTED CV

I hope this book has been helpful.

This is the first edition of *Become a Part-time Professor*.

If you have questions or feedback, please email me at lesa@parttimeprofessor.com.

...and I love to hear success stories.

I look forward to hearing from you.

Remember to visit HTTP://PARTTIMEPROFESSOR.COM

IF YOU WOULD LIKE A COMPLIMENTARY COPY OF THE EBOOK WITH LINKS, EMAIL ME.